LEWIS GUN MECHANISM MADE EASY

I0191257

By

MAJOR C. H. B. PRIDHAM
The Duke of Wellington's Regiment
(*Late Officer-Instructor, School of Musketry, Hythe*)

SIXTH EDITION

WITH NOTES ON
THE .300 (AMERICAN) LEWIS GUN

The Naval & Military Press Ltd
© 2008

Published by the

The Naval & Military Press

in association with the Royal Armouries

Unit 10 Ridgewood Industrial Park,
Uckfield, East Sussex, TN22 5QE
Tel: +44 (0) 1825 749494
Fax: +44 (0) 1825 765701

MILITARY HISTORY AT YOUR FINGERTIPS
www.naval-military-press.com

ONLINE GENEALOGY RESEARCH
www.military-genealogy.com

ONLINE MILITARY CARTOGRAPHY
www.militarymaproom.com

ROYAL
ARMOURIES

The Library & Archives Department at the
Royal Armouries Museum, Leeds, specialises
in the history and development of armour
and weapons from earliest times to the
present day. Material relating to the
development of artillery and modern
fortifications is held at the Royal
Armouries Museum, Fort Nelson.

For further information contact:
Royal Armouries Museum, Library, Armouries Drive,
Leeds, West Yorkshire LS10 1LT
Royal Armouries, Library, Fort Nelson, Down End Road, Fareham PO17 6AN

Or visit the Museum's website at
www.armouries.org.uk

PREFACE TO REVISED EDITION
(NOVEMBER, 1940)

RAPID TRAINING

THIS handbook for Lewis Gunners (1st Edition in 1919) was the first of its kind to supplement the old official textbooks, which were not specially adapted for rapid training purposes.

Method of arrangement (**Text** and **Diagrams**) is intended :

(a) To **Save Time** in **Training.**

(b) To arouse **interest** in the gunner, with a view to increasing his **skill** in rapidly applying accurate bursts of fire on to any target.

Text has been set out to **catch the eye.**

The intricate design of the mechanism is thus made clear to the understanding of any sailor, soldier, airman-gunner, or A.A. gunner of the Mercantile Marine or Mine-Sweeping Flotillas, Auxiliary Military Pioneer Corps, and The Home Guard, whose time available for Lewis Gun training is limited by his other numerous duties.

Care of Arms.—Experience in action shows the great importance of this old subject. A thorough knowledge of **mechanism**, particularly fascinating in the case of the Lewis Gun, ensures this.

Cooling System.—A unique feature is the Cooling of the Barrel (see page 10 and Fig. III), **the most effective system of Air Cooling ever invented.**

This enables the Lewis Gun to fire, at a rate of 10 rounds per second, for a prolonged period.

No Barrel Changing is necessary.

Diagrams (at end of book) can be **spread out** and examined whilst reading the text.

IMPORTANT. — Faulty (foreign manufactured) ammunition has, in the past, been the main cause of **STOPPAGES.** Proper care of the Gun (see pages 12 and 18) and use of good ammunition (of British make) reduce Stoppages to a minimum.

C. H. B. PRIDHAM (*Major*).

CONTENTS

LEWIS GUN MECHANISM MADE EASY

I

"The .303 (and the .300 American type) Light Automatic Gun—Air cooled—Gas operated—Magazine fed." **Description of GUN.**

Weight of Gun : 26 to 28 lbs. ; Weight of Mounting, 2¾ lbs.

Weight of Magazine : Empty, 1½ lbs. ; full 4⅛ lbs. (Holds 47 rounds.)*

Length of Gun : 50½ inches.

Length of Barrel : 26¼ inches.

Initial Velocity of Bullet : 2,440 feet per second.

Two forces work the Gun automatically, viz. :

1. The pressure of the **Gases,** caused by explosion of the Charge.

2. **The Return Spring,** contained in the Pinion.

These two forces alone enable the Gun to fire at an average rate of ten rounds per second.

A trained Lewis Gunner should be able to fire with accuracy 150 rounds per minute.

The Position of the Cocking Handle normally shows whether the Gun is " Safe " or Loaded—*i.e.,* when a Filled Magazine is in position on the Gun :—

> A. When C.H. is fully forward (*vide* Fig. II) —Gun is " Safe."

---

* Note.—Magazines (double-sized, holding about **94** rounds) are also in use by the Royal Navy and the R.A.F.

B. When C.H. is in rear position (*vide* Fig. I) —Gun is Loaded.

Note that when Gun is not in use, C.H. should be always in Forward Position, to avoid unnecessary strain or tension on the Return Spring.

II

To LOAD. 1. See that Cocking Handle is in Forward Position.

2. Place **Filled Magazine** on the Magazine Post —Catch to Right—White of Centre Disc to Rear ; press down Magazine, and at the same time rotate slightly in both directions without undue force, till the Hook of the Catch engages in the Recess inside the Magazine Post.

3. Rotate **Magazine** with Right Hand until resistance is met with.

4. **Pull back C.H.** to rear as far as it will go.*

(N.B.—This action places a Live Round in position in the Cartridge Way in the Body by action of the Feed-Arm and Cartridge Guide, ready to be pushed forward by the Bolt into the Chamber— *vide* Fig. I.)

GUN is Now READY to FIRE.

To FIRE. A. *If Trigger is Pressed*—Gun fires.

B. *If pressure on Trigger is released*—C.H. will stop in the Rear Position, and Gun is Loaded and ready to continue firing, by Nose of Sear being engaged with Bent on Rack.

C. *If pressure on Trigger is maintained*, and Gun ceases to fire owing to Empty Magazine—

---

* NOTE.—The .300 (American type) Lewis Gun has Cocking Handle on left side of Body. To pull back Cocking Handle left hand must therefore be used

C.H. will be in Forward Position, and Gun will be Unloaded Automatically.

(N.B.—**An Empty Magazine rotates freely on the Gun.** If resistance is met with, this is caused by a Live Round coming up against the Cartridge Stop on the Feed Arm.)

EMPTY MAGAZINE.

———

III

A. **NORMAL—viz., at a Firing Position** or when Front is clear.

1. Remove Magazine.

2. Raise Butt into shoulder and press Trigger, and repeat (*i.e.*, pull back C.H. and press Trigger) for safety.

Gun is now Automatically Unloaded.

To UNLOAD Normal.

———

B. **WITHOUT FIRING, or when CHAMBER is not Clear.**

1. Pull back C.H.

2. Remove Magazine.

3. *Depress Base of Live Round under Cartridge Guide* with Point of Bullet (or Stripping Tool), and draw Bullet of Round forward until its Point rests above Opening in Feed Arm.

4. *Hold C.H. back with Right Hand; press Trigger with Left,* and allow C.H. to come half-way forward. Bolt will then tap Base of Round clear of Cartridge Guide and underneath Cartridge Stop.

Pull back C.H. to full extent, and release pressure on Trigger. Round can now be removed easily.

To UNLOAD WITHOUT FIRING.

5. Press Trigger.

(N.B.—Above is the method recommended for Unloading without Firing.)

IV

ACTION of MECHANISM described in detail,

giving Names of each Part and how they Function.

All Parts shown in the Diagrams I, II and III, and in the other Diagrams, are numbered alike.

ACTION of MECHANISM during the BACKWARD MOVEMENT.

Action of GASES. When a round is fired, the gases force the **Bullet (1)** up the barrel : a portion of them escapes through the **Gas-Vent (2)** into the **Gas* Chamber (3)** and **Gas Regulator (4)**,* thence into the **Gas Cylinder (5)**, where they strike against the **PISTON ROD.** **Head (6) of the Piston Rod,** forcing the **Piston Rod (7)** to the rear.

Action of RETURN SPRING. As the Piston Rod travels backwards the **Teeth on the Rack (8)**, being engaged with the **Teeth on the Pinion (9)**, rotate the Pinion and wind up the **Return Spring (10)**.

STRIKER POST. The **Striker Post (11)**, being one with the Piston Rod, and situated inside the **Cam Slot (12)**, moves back a distance of 1½ inches along the straight portion of the Cam Slot.

SAFETY LOCKING DEVICE. (N.B.—This is a device to insure Locking of the Bolt until the Bullet is clear of the Muzzle.)

---

* NOTE.—Gas Chamber of .300 Gun has also a Gas Chamber Gland. Gas Regulator has 4 holes (Nos. 1, 2, 3, 4) varying in size. .303 Gun has 2 holes only. Smallest hole that gives sufficient gas should be used.

Backward
Movement
(*continued*)
BOLT and
LOCKING
LUGS.

The Rear of the Striker Post then presses against the **Curved Part** (13) of the Cam Slot and rotates the **Bolt** (14) to the Left, thus releasing the **Lugs** (15) on the Bolt from the **Locking Recesses** (16) in the Body.

The Lugs are now clear of the Recesses and in line with the **Guide Grooves** (17), which run along the inside of the Body. The Rear of the Striker Post then comes against the Rear end of the Cam Slot, and the Piston Rod, continuing on its backward travel, thus carries the Bolt to the Rear.

(NOTE.—**When the TRIGGER is pressed,** the Piston Rod is able to run free during both Backward and Forward Movements—*i.e.*, the **Bent** (18) behind the Rack passes over the **Nose** (19) of the **Sear** (20), which is kept depressed. **When the TRIGGER is released** the Bent rides over the Nose of the Sear towards the end of the Backward Movement ; when the Bent has passed, the Sear rises again under the influence of the *Trigger Spring (21), and engages with the Bent directly after the commencement of the Forward Movement.)

The two **Extractors** (22) on the Bolt withdraw the **Empty Case** (23) from the **Chamber** (24) (*vide* Fig. III).

The **Left Lug** (25) (*vide* Fig. VI) on the **Rear End of the Bolt** (26) moving to the Rear, pushes the **Tail** (27) of the **Ejector** (28) out of the Boltway, and, the Ejector being pivoted, the **Head** (29) swings in and ejects the Empty Case through the Ejection Slot.

The **Feed Arm Actuating Stud** (30), working in the **Grooved Tail** (31) of the **Feed Arm** (32),

* NOTE.—The .300 Gun has the Spring fitted to the Sear, and not to the Trigger, as in the .303 Gun.

carries the Feed Arm across to the Left (*vide* Fig. IV).

FEED ARM PAWL. The **Feed Arm Pawl** (33), being engaged behind a **Projection** (34) on the Magazine, and being carried across with the Feed Arm, thus rotates the Magazine one space to the Left.

**MAGAZINE.
(Mechanism,
vide
Fig. VIII.)** In the Magazine a Live Round is forced down the Slope of the Centre Block until the Bullet end is clear of the Lip, when it drops on to the Body and into the Cartridge Opening in the Feed Arm, being assisted down by the **Projecting Tongue (35)** of the Body Cover.

**LIVE
ROUND.** The Round is carried to the Left (and forced into position under the Cartridge Guide) by the **Indentations** (36) and **Separating Pegs** (37) in the Magazine, assisted by the Right Side of the Cartridge Opening in the Feed Arm.

**No. 2
(RIGHT)
STOP
PAWL.** The **Feed Arm Pawl Spring Retaining Stud** (38), moving to the Left across the Face of the **No. 2 (Right) Stop Pawl** (39), allows the latter to come forward [under the influence of the **Stop Pawl Spring (40)**] and engage in front of a **Projection** (41) on the Magazine, thus preventing the Magazine from rotating too far in the feeding direction.

**No. 1
(LEFT)
STOP
PAWL.** The **No. 1 (Left) Stop Pawl** (42) is pressed back as a Projection on the Magazine rides over it, but it comes forward again when the Projection is clear and engages behind it, thus preventing the Magazine from counter rotating.

**FEED ARM
TAIL STUD.** At the end of the Backward Movement the Feed Arm Actuating Stud disengages from the

Grooved Tail of the Feed Arm, which is held in
position ready for the next Forward Movement
by the Positioning Stud on the tail of the Feed
Arm engaging with the Left Side of the Top
Locking Lug on the Bolt.

***

V

ACTION of MECHANISM during FORWARD MOVEMENT.

Forward Movement. Action of—

[For Position of Mechanism at commencement of
Forward Movement, see Fig. I.]

When the Gun is Cocked the Return Spring is
held compressed by the **Nose (19)** of the **Sear (20)**,
being engaged in the **Bent (18)** in rear of the Rack
on the Piston Rod.

SEAR and BENT.

On pressing the Trigger, the Nose of the Sear
is released from the Bent, and the **Return Spring
(10)** comes into play and rotates the **Pinion (9)**.

PINION and RETURN SPRING.

The Teeth of the Pinion being engaged with
the **Teeth on the Rack (8)**, the **Piston Rod (7)** is
driven forward.

The **Striker Post (11)**, being now held in the
Rear end of the **Cam Slot (13)** in the **Bolt (14)**,
tries to rotate the Bolt, but cannot, owing to the
Lugs (15), which are prevented from turning in
the **Guide Grooves (17)**.

STRIKER POST and BOLT.

The Bolt is therefore carried forward by the
Striker Post.

***

The **Feed Arm Actuating Stud (30)** is also car-
ried forward with the Bolt, and, riding inside the
Grooved Tail (31) of the Feed Arm, carries the
Feed Arm (32) over to the Right (*vide* Fig. V).

F.A.S. and FEED ARM.

Forward Movement *(continued)*

FEED ARM PAWL. The **Feed Arm Pawl** (**33**) during this movement passes over a projection on the Magazine, and engages behind it.

No. 2 (RIGHT) STOP PAWL. The **Feed Arm Pawl Spring Retaining Stud** (**38**) on the Feed Arm, moving to the Right, presses back the **No. 2 (Right) Stop Pawl** (**39**) out of the way of the Magazine.

No. 1 (LEFT) STOP PAWL. The **No. 1 (Left) Stop Pawl** (**42**) remains stationary, preventing the Magazine from rebounding or being drawn back by the Feed Arm Pawl.

TOP EXTRACTOR and BOLT. During the Forward Movement of the Bolt the **Top Extractor** (**43**) meets the Rim of the Cartridge, and pushes it forwards and downwards, into the Chamber, the Cartridge being guided and con-

CARTRIDGE GUIDE, CARTRIDGE and BULLET STOPS. trolled during this movement by the **Cartridge Guide** (**44**), **Cartridge** (**45**) and **Bullet Stops** (**46**) on the Feed Arm and the Shoulders of the Cartridge Slot in the Body.

BOLT. The face of the Bolt knocks the **Head of the Ejector** (**29**) out of the Boltway, and the Tail (**27**) swings in behind ready for the Backward Movement.

EXTRACTORS. The Extractors spring over the Rim of the Cartridge as it goes into the Chamber.

The Bolt is now forward to the full extent; the **Lugs** (**15**) are clear of the Guide Grooves and opposite the **Locking Recesses** (**16**) in the Body.

STRIKER POST. The **Striker Post** (**11**) is now able to rotate the Bolt to the Right, and the Lugs enter the **Locking Recesses** (**16**), thus locking the Bolt.

Forward
Movement
(*continued*)

The Striker Post meanwhile has pushed its way through the **Curved Portion** (**13**) of the Cam Slot, and it now enters the straight portion.

STRIKER.

The **Striker** (**47**) travels along the straight portion, its nose passes through the Striker Way in the face of the Bolt, hits the Cap, and explodes the Charge.

VI

MECHANISM of the MAGAZINE and Functions of PARTS.

See **Fig. VIII**
Diagrams
1 to 7.

I.—The MAGAZINE consists of :—

(A) Circular Rotating Pan, and—

(B) Inner Ring.

These are riveted together and rotate around—

(C) The Centre Block of Aluminium, and—

(D) The Centre Disc with Catch and Spring.

These are also riveted together, but remain stationary.

II.—When the MAGAZINE is not in use :—

MAGAZINE
off the GUN.

1. Nib on the end of the Catch is engaged in one of the twenty-five recesses of the Inner Ring, which also carries the Separating Pegs.

2. This prevents the Pan from rotating around the Centre Block, except when a loading Handle has been inserted into the Central Opening or Axis Hole for the purpose of Filling.

III.—When a Filled MAGAZINE is fixed on the GUN :—

MAGAZINE
on the GUN.

1. Magazine Catch is forced to the Right by the Hollow Cone of the Magazine Post ; this disengages the Nib from the Recess on the Inner Ring, and frees the Pan from the Centre Disc.

MAGAZINE on the GUN *(continued)* 2. The Pan is now able to rotate, and the Centre Block is forced to remain stationary by the Key on the exterior of the Magazine Post, which fits into the Keyway on the Centre Block.

3. The Pan rotating with the Inner Ring around the Centre Block causes a round to be carried by the Indentations and Separating Pegs free of the Lip at the end of the Spiral Channel in which the Bullet end lies.

4. The Round then falls out, being ensured falling by the Tongue of the Body Cover.

VII

GASES and COOLING SYSTEM. **ACTION of GASES and COOLING SYSTEM** (*vide* Fig. III).

When a Round has been fired, the Bullet is forced up the Barrel by the Gases which pass out of the Muzzle and expand, striking against the Cone-shaped Interior of the **Barrel Mouthpiece (48)**, which concentrates them and increases their pressure.

Passing out of the Barrel Mouthpiece, they meet, rebound, and strike against the **Fore Radiator Casing (49)** (about 1½ inches from the end), expelling all the Air in front of them.

This causes Suction behind them, and draws Cool Air through the **Flanges (50) of the Radiator.**

The Radiator, being made of Aluminium, which is a good conductor of Heat, and being in close contact with the Barrel throughout its length, quickly draws the Heat from the Barrel, and thus cools the Gun.

(N.B.—Note the shape of the Fore Radiator Casing, which is tapered, and thus assists in expelling the Air and increasing the Suction.)

NOTE.—The .300 (American type) Lewis Gun—as issued to the Home Guard—has *no Radiator or Radiator Casing,* and is therefore similar in appearance to the Lewis Gun as used by the R.A.F.

VIII

1. *Withdraw Pistol Grip with Right Hand,* thereby allowing Pinion Pawl to engage in Teeth of Pinion. At the same time—

2. *With the Left Hand press up Pinion Casing,* so that the Teeth of the Pinion are engaged with the Teeth on the Rack.

3. *Draw back Cocking Handle* the required distance.

4. *Release Pinion, and replace C.H.* in the forward position.

5. Reassemble Pinion and Pistol Grip.

6. Weigh Return Spring with the Spring Balance.

To INCREASE TENSION of RETURN SPRING.

———

(NOTE.—*Care must be taken to hold Pinion up tight* while drawing back C.H. by placing left thumb over top of Body and fingers under Pinion Casing, or damage may be done to the Teeth of Rack or Pinion. To avoid possibility of this occurring when adding considerable Weight, pull back C.H. about 2 inches only two or three times.)

———

1. *Withdraw Pistol Grip and allow Pinion Casing to drop,* so as to disengage Pinion with Rack.

2. *Draw back C.H.* the required distance (1 inch gives 2 to 3 lbs.).

3. *Press up Pinion Casing* (with Left Hand) to engage Pinion with Rack.

4. *Push Pistol Grip home* to connect with Pinion Pawl; Piston Rod then flies forward, and Rack unwinds Return Spring.

5. Reassemble and Weigh Return Spring.

To DECREASE TENSION of RETURN SPRING.

I.—POINTS which should always be carried out BEFORE FIRING.

1. Remove oil from Bore and Gas Cylinder (if oily). All gas parts to be **absolutely** dry.

2. Oil all Frictional Parts behind Body Locking Pin, and smear Bolt and Striker Post with graphite grease.

3. Weigh and adjust Return Spring (normally 12 to 14 lbs. with C.H. in Forward Position).

4. Test Feed Mechanism (*i.e.*, the Pawls).

5. Make sure that Barrel Mouthpiece and Clamp Ring are screwed up tight.

6. Examine Magazines and Ammunition when filling.

7. Examine Spare Parts and adjust Spare Return Spring to same tension as that on the Gun.

8. Examine Mounting to see whether in good order, correctly fixed on, and firm in the ground.

II.—POINTS DURING FIRING—*i.e.*, to be carried out during a Temporary Cessation of Fire.

1. Replace empty Magazines in carriers, and send back for Refilling.

2. Slightly Oil as in Point 2 (" Before Firing "), especially Bolt, Striker Post, and Magazine Post (owing to Heat caused by firing).

3. See that Clamp Ring is tightly screwed up.

4. Examine and, if necessary, adjust Mounting.

5. Turn Gas Regulator slightly to prevent " seizing " of threads.

6. Weigh Return Spring.

7. Place a Full Magazine on the Gun and Reload.

III.—**POINTS** to be carried out **AFTER FIRING.**

1. **Immediately after FIRING :—**
   (1) Unload and clear Gun.
   (2) Release Tension off the Return Spring.
   (3) Clean Barrel, leaving Oily.

2. **In Billets or after return from Firing :—**
   (4) Strip down Gun, clean thoroughly, and Oil. (Clean Barrel with Boiling Water, if available.)
   (5) Clean and scrape Fouling off Gas Chamber, and all Gas parts.
   (6) Examine, dry and Oil Magazines.
   (7) Examine and Clean Mounting.
   (8) Carry out any necessary Repairs.
   (9) Clean Barrel thoroughly daily for at least ten days, leaving Oily.
   (10) Enter up approximate number of Rounds fired, Breakages, and number of Barrel used in Gun's History Sheet.

————

CARE and CLEANING Notes.

1. Never put too much Oil on the Frictional Parts, as they work better with a little, especially in cold weather.

2. Oil in Gas Cylinder causes Fouling, and renders Gun very liable to Frictional Stoppages.

3. To clean Gas Parts, use Mineral Burning Oil (Paraffin) ; this will reduce Fouling Stoppages to a minimum.

4. Clean Gun daily in damp climates ; weekly in dry atmospheres.

5. In Gas affected areas, or where Gun has been sprayed with Gas, clean thoroughly with Petrol or Paraffin. Burn all rags used.

X

NOTES on STOPPAGES.

1. In common with other Automatic Guns, the Lewis Gun is liable to Accidental Cessation of Fire or Stoppages.

The object of the Lewis Gunner is to get the Gun firing again in the shortest possible time.

---

2. Roughly, about 90 per cent. of all Stoppages can be rectified at once by the application of what is known as " Immediate Action." Others can be remedied quickly by Examination of the Gun, a thorough knowledge of Mechanism, and practice in rectifying Stoppages.

---

3. STOPPAGES may be either TEMPORARY or PROLONGED.

(1) Temporary : Those which can be cured by Immediate Action ; these are generally *due to neglect of the Points to be observed Before, During or After Firing.*

(2) Prolonged : These involving stripping down the Gun to remove a jamb caused by Breakage, or to rectify any failure in the Mechanism which cannot usually be carried out under Fire, and which put the Gun out of Action for a more or less prolonged period.

4. In any STOPPAGE the COCKING HANDLE stops in one of two different POSITIONS, known as :—

1st Position   ...   C.H. is fully forward.
2nd Position   ...   C.H. in any position **between 1st** (as above) and Gun fully cocked.

Knowledge of the Causes of Stoppage peculiar to each position, and how to rectify them in the shortest possible time, is essential.

N.B.—These Positions can be quickly determined by **TOUCH**, as follows :—

With Butt in Shoulder, raise Fingers (extended) of Right Hand straight up from the Pistol Grip. **POSITION FOUND BY TOUCH.**

If C.H. is felt at the Tips of the Fingers—1st Position.

If C.H. is felt on any other part of the Hand—2nd Position.

---

5. **When STRIPPING a GUN to clear a STOPPAGE,** take care not to alter the Tension on the Return Spring. Whenever possible, see that C.H. is **forward** before removing or replacing Pistol Grip. **NOTE ON STRIPPING.**

Correct way to remove the Bolt.—Take off Butt—Hold up Pinion with Left Hand—Disengage Pistol Grip—Drop Pinion—Pull out Piston Rod.

Caution.—Bolt will not go into Boltway if—

(1) Tail of Ejector protrudes into Boltway.

(2) Rear End of Bolt is not properly screwed up.

---

6. **To remove a Separated Case from the Chamber,** use of the Clearing Plug is necessary, as follows :— **HOW TO USE CLEARING PLUG.**

To remove Separated Case:—

(1) Insert tapered end of Clearing Plug into Chamber, **with centre pin pushed back**.

(2) Press Trigger, allowing Bolt to force centre pin forward.

(3) Give Clearing Plug Handle an up-and-down rocking motion.

HOW TO USE CLEARING PLUG
(continued)

(4) Pull back C.H., and withdraw Clearing Plug from Chamber.

(5) Press Trigger, load, and carry on Firing.

(6) To remove Separation from Clearing Plug, knock centre pin back.

IMMEDIATE ACTION.

IMMEDIATE ACTION.

7. Definition.—The initial attempt to remedy the Stoppage and get the Gun firing again as quickly as possible.

First—Always feel for Position of Cocking Handle.

(1) *If in 1st Position.*—Rotate Magazine— Pull back C.H.—Relay Gun, and carry on Firing.

(2) *If in 2nd Position.*—Pull back C.H.— Counter-rotate Magazine—Relay Gun, and carry on Firing.

This application of Immediate Action must be practised until it becomes a habit. It should be Instantaneous and Automatic.

FURTHER ACTION.

8. If IMMEDIATE ACTION fails to remedy the STOPPAGE, proceed at once to apply any further Action that may be necessary to get the Gun firing again, as follows :—

After application of IMMEDIATE ACTION— Again Feel for Position of Cocking Handle.

(1) *C.H. again stops in 1st Position.*—Proceed to—

    (*a*) Remove Magazine.

    (*b*) Examine Feed Mechanism (*i.e.*, the Pawls).

    (*c*) Pull back C.H., and examine Striker.

(2) *C.H. again stops in 2nd Position.*—Proceed to—

    (*a*) Pull back C.H.

    (*b*) Remove Magazine.

    (*c*) Examine Chamber, Ejection Opening, Cartridge Slot and Guide.

FURTHER ACTION (*continued*)

Any further Action which may still be necessary will be found in the **TABLE OF STOPPAGES** (Columns 4 and 6).

———

9. The following **TABLE OF STOPPAGES** (pages 19 and 20) is arranged in **TWO Sections** :—

    (A) Giving **PROBABLE STOPPAGES,** which are cured by **IMMEDIATE ACTION,** and—

    (B) Giving **POSSIBLE STOPPAGES,** for which **FURTHER ACTION** is necessary.

EXPLANATION OF TABLE OF STOPPAGES.

First—*Learn how to recognize and rectify all Stoppages in Section A* before proceeding to Section B. *Those in Section B should occur very seldom.*

Column 1 shows Position of Cocking Handle.

Column 2 emphasizes the importance of Immediate Action.

Column 3 gives the Result of Applying Immediate Action.

Column 4 shows How to Remedy the Stoppage.

Column 5 indicates the Cause of the Stoppage,

Column 6 gives any Further Action or Information not already indicated.

The Abbreviations " I.A." and " C.H." indicate Immediate Action and Cocking Handle respectively.

18

STOP-PAGES. How Arranged.
10. **STOPPAGES in the TABLE** are numbered consecutively, and arranged—

(1) According to Position of Cocking Handle.

(2) In order of Probability.

Note.—Order of Probability of Stoppages in the TABLE was originally compiled as a result of experience gained in the War of 1915-18, on many fronts. From 1915 onwards, and for many years afterwards, vast quantities of Ammunition of Faulty (Foreign) Manufacture were used, causing Breakages, Blowbacks and Burst Cases.

IMPORT-ANCE OF GOOD AMMUNI-TION.
11. With good Ammunition of British make, **very few Stoppages that are not cured by Immediate Action** should be incurred—especially if the Points Before, During, and After Firing are duly carried out.

STOPPAGES during the PRESENT WAR.
According to information recently received (October, 1940) extremely few Stoppages are now incurred.

MULTIPLE LEWIS GUNS.
12. The use of Lewis Guns in pairs (preferably used alternately), or in multiple form, increases Volume of Fire and also minimises the importance of Stoppages.

TABLE A. PROBABLE STOPPAGES—CURED BY IMMEDIATE ACTION.

No.	1. Position of C.H.	2. Action.	3. Result of Applying Immediate Action.	4. Stoppage—How Remedied.	5. Cause of Stoppage.	6. Remarks.
1.	1st	I.A.	Magazine rotates freely : No Feed	Change Magazine	Empty Magazine	—
2.	1st	I.A.	Gun Fires	Cured by I.A.	Misfire : Defective Round	If it recurs—Change Magazine.
3.	1st	I.A.	Magazine does not rotate : no Feed. Gun does not Fire	Change Magazine	Misfeed— Damaged or Worn Magazine	N.B.—Liable to occur under War conditions.
4.	2nd	I.A. (using Lanyard)	Gun Fires	Cured by I.A.	Hard Extraction (Faulty Ammunition)	Cartridge Case unduly expanded in Chamber, or Bulged Round.
5.	2nd	I.A. (using Lanyard)	Gun does not Fire : Obstruction in Chamber prevents Live Round from entering	Cured by I.A.— i.e., if separation comes out on Empty Case pulled back by Lanyard	Separated Case (Faulty Ammunition)	N.B.—If not cured by I.A., use of Clearing Plug is necessary (See No. 11, Table B).
6.	2nd	I.A.	Gun may or may not Fire : or Fires a few Rounds, and stops again	Cured by I.A. (if not, see Remarks Col.)	Excessive Friction or Fouling	If it recurs—(a) Oil frictional parts as in Points "Before." (b) Take 3 lb. weight off Return Spring.
7.	2nd	I.A.	Gun Fires	Cured by I.A.	Fault in Feed	If it recurs—Change Cartridge Guide.
8.	Any	I.A.	Little or no Tension in pulling back C.H.	Change Pinion*	Broken Return Spring	Rare Stoppage.

* N.B.—Pinions of .303 and .300 types Lewis Gun are not interchangeable.   Latter type is to be painted with a red band.

TABLE B. POSSIBLE STOPPAGES—FOR WHICH FURTHER ACTION IS NECESSARY.

No.	1. Position of C.H.	2. Action.	3. Result of Applying Immediate Action.	4. Stoppage—How Remedied.	5. Cause of Stoppage.	6. Remarks.
9.	1st	I.A.	Gun does not Fire: nothing Ejected: Magazine does not rotate: No Feed	Change Feed Arm Pawl Spring	Broken or Weak Feed Arm Pawl Spring	Fault usually found in Spring. But Feed Arm Pawl may be worn.
10.	1st	I.A.	Gun does not Fire: Feed Mechanism correct: Live Round Ejected	Change Piston Rod	Broken or Faulty Striker	—
11.	2nd	I.A. (using Lanyard)	Gun does not Fire: Obstruction in Chamber prevents Live Round from entering	Obstruction removed with Clearing Plug	Separated Case (jammed in Chamber)	If Clearing Plug* not available — Reload, press Trigger, and Obstruction may adhere to next Round.
12.	2nd	I.A.	Gun stops again: Live Round jammed against Empty in Chamber	Clear Gun, and Change Bolt	Broken, Worn or Gritty Extractor	N.B.—Remove broken piece, or No. 14 Prolonged Stop. may result. Broken Bottom Extractor is liable to cause No. 14 Stoppage.
13.	2nd	I.A.	Empty Case in Bolt-way prevents Bolt from feeding Live Round into Chamber	Clear Gun, and carry on Firing	Faulty Ejection	If it recurs—Change Ejector.
14.	2nd	I.A.	Mechanism jammed: Obstruction in Bolt-way	Strip down Gun, and remove	Broken piece of Metal in Bolt-way	Prolonged Stop. resulting from Breakage: broken part jammed in Mechanism.
15.	2nd	I.A.	Double Feed	Clear Gun, and Change (Right) Stop Pawl	Faulty Action of Stop Pawl	Caused by dirt, or Worn Pawl.

NOTE.—If Clearing Plug is not available, and SEPARATION does not adhere to next round—Increase TENSION on RETURN SPRING, and repeat.
(See instructions on how to use Clearing Plug, on page 15, para. 6.)

FIG. IV.
POSITION of FEED ARM and PAWLS at commencement of BACKWARD MOVEMENT.

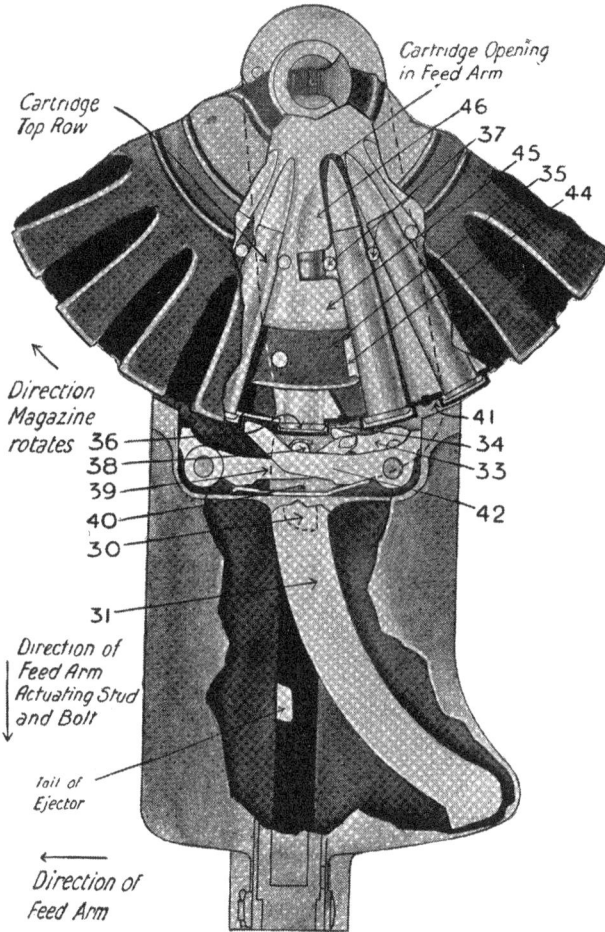

Cartridge Opening
in Feed Arm

Cartridge
Top Row

46

37

45

35

44

Direction
Magazine
rotates

36

38

39

40

30

41

34

33

42

31

Direction of
Feed Arm
Actuating Stud
and Bolt

Tail of
Ejector

Direction of
Feed Arm

FIG. V.
POSITION of FEED ARM and PAWLS at end of BACKWARD MOVEMENT.

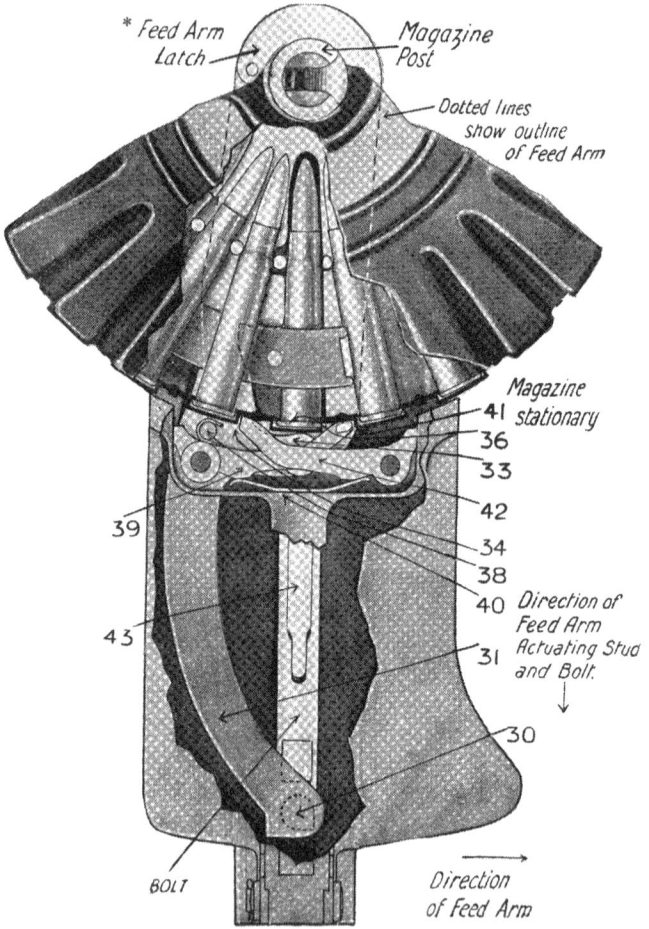

* Feed Arm Latch

Magazine Post

Dotted lines show outline of Feed Arm

Magazine stationary — 41

36

33

42

34

38

40 — Direction of Feed Arm Actuating Stud and Bolt.

31

30

39

43

BOLT

Direction of Feed Arm

*N.B.—Applies to .303 Gun only.

FIG. Va.

THE FEED ARM.
Giving Names of Parts.

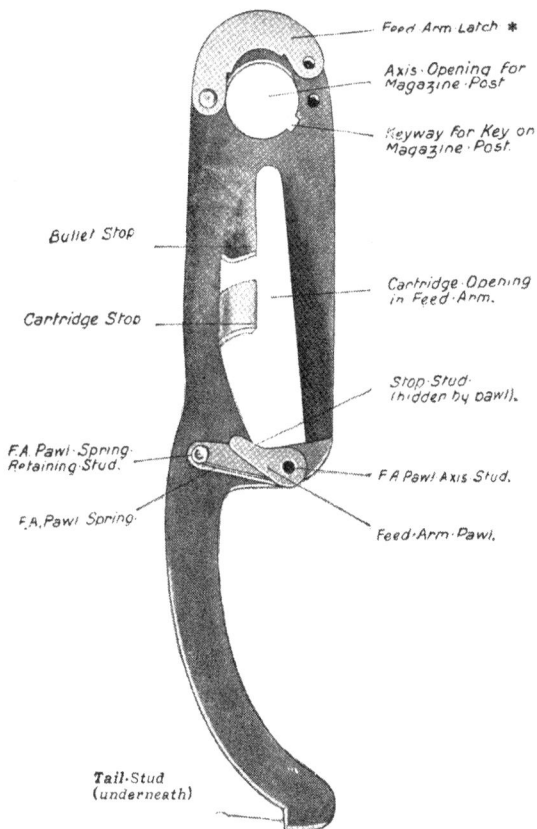

Feed Arm Latch *

Axis Opening for Magazine Post

Keyway for Key on Magazine Post.

Bullet Stop

Cartridge Opening in Feed Arm.

Cartridge Stop

Stop Stud (hidden by pawl).

F.A. Pawl Spring Retaining Stud.

F.A. Pawl Axis Stud.

F.A. Pawl Spring.

Feed Arm Pawl.

Tail Stud (underneath)

*N.B.—Applies to .303 Gun only.   .300 Gun has a Tongue fitting under a Recess in front of the Body.

FIG. VI.

Action of EJECTOR during BACKWARD MOVEMENT.

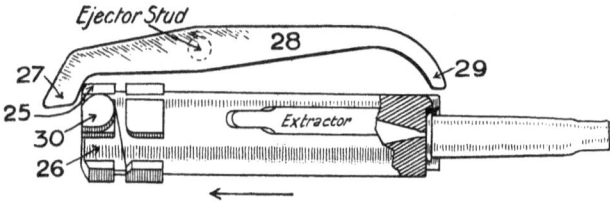

Diagram A.—Position Before Ejection of Empty Case.

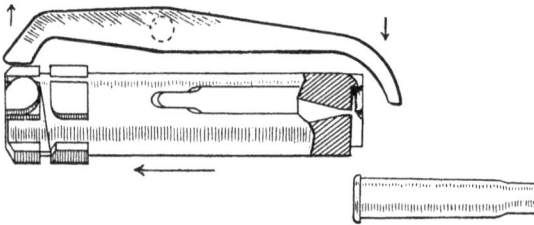

Diagram B.—Position After Ejection of Empty Case.

FIG. VII.

Action of STRIKER POST in CAM SLOT.

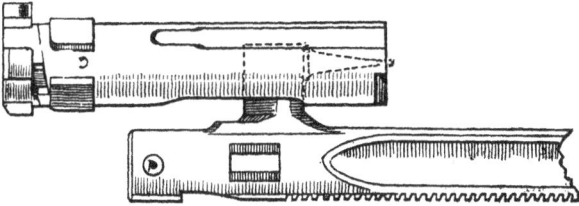

Diagram A.—AT END OF FORWARD MOVEMENT.
STRIKER POST in Straight Portion of SLOT.

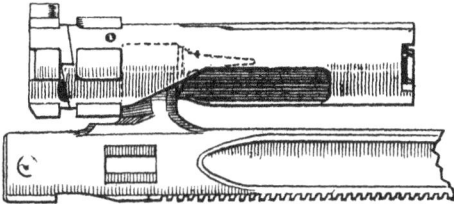

Diagram B.—DURING BACKWARD MOVEMENT.
STRIKER POST in Rear End of Curved Portion of SLOT
having Rotated BOLT to the Left.

No. 1.

No. 2.

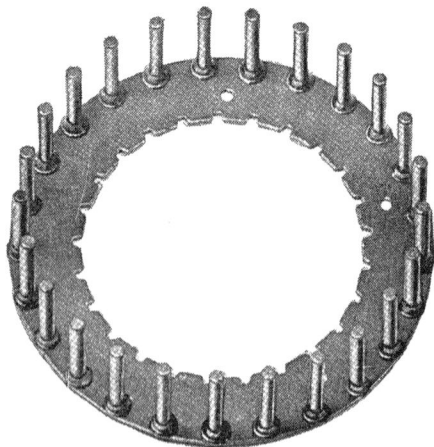

No. 3.

No. 4.

No. 5.

No. 6.

No. 7.

FIG. VIII (See Pages 9 and 10).

Diagram 1 showing (A) Magazine **Pan.**

Diagram 2 showing (B) Inner **Ring, with 25 Separating Pegs** and **Recesses.***

Diagram 3 showing the **Pan** and **Ring** riveted together, showing how **Round** is held in position by **Rim Plates** and **Separating Pegs.**

Diagram 4 showing (C) **Centre Block** of Aluminium, showing **Spiral Channel, Ramp,** and **Lip** for **Bullet** end of round ; also **Key Way** and **Central Opening.**

Diagram 5 showing (D) **Centre Disc, Catch,** and **Spring.**

Diagram 6 showing **Centre Disc**—top view. Note portion painted **White.**

Diagram 7 showing **Magazine** with **Centre Disc** removed.

*N.B.—Double-sized Magazines are also in use. (See page 1.)

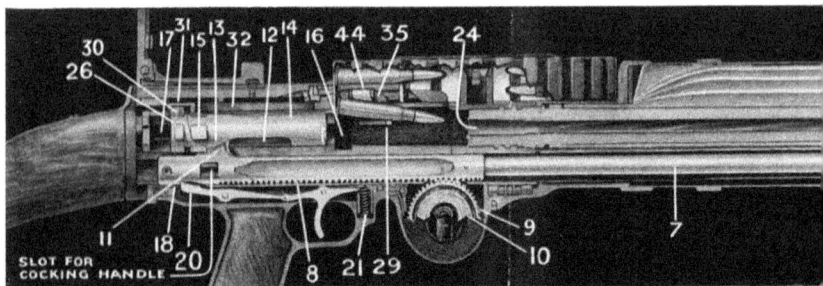

Fig. I

shows LEWIS GUN loaded and ready to FIRE.

Cocking Handle is in Rear Position. Live Round is held in position under **Cartridge Guide** (**44**), resting on shoulders of Cartridge Slot in the Body. **Return Spring** (**10**) is held compressed owing to Nose of Sear being engaged in Bent behind Rack of Piston Rod.

———

Fig. II

shows position of MECHANISM the moment after STRIKER (47) has exploded CHARGE.

Cocking Handle is in Forward Position. **Bullet** (**1**) has been forced down Barrel by the pressure of the Gases. Breech is locked to take the force of the explosion.

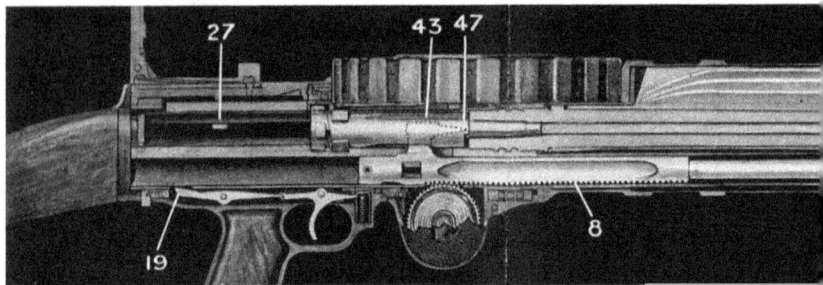

———

Fig. III

shows the BACKWARD MOVEMENT of the MECHANISM in progress, and Action of the GASES operating the COOLING SYSTEM.

Bullet has left the Muzzle. A portion of the Gases has entered the **Gas Vent** (**2**), passed through **Gas Chamber** (**3**), and into **Gas Cylinder** (**5**), thus forcing **Piston Rod** (**7**) to the Rear. This action has unlocked the Breech, and is winding up Return Spring. The Bolt, moving to the Rear, has extracted the **Empty Case** (**23**), which is about to be ejected through Ejection Slot.

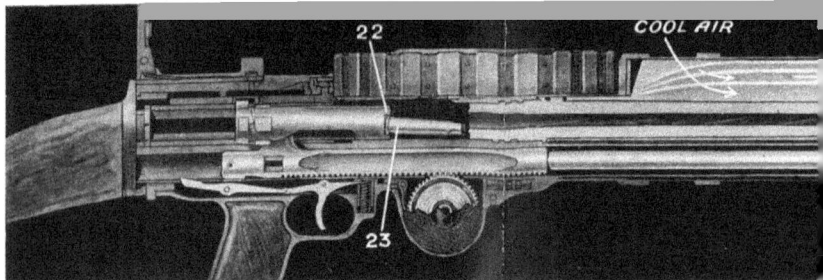

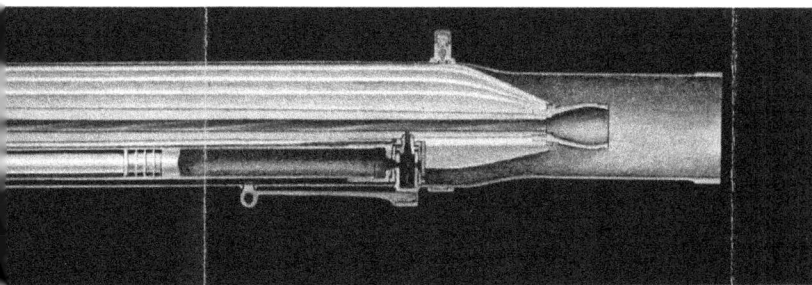

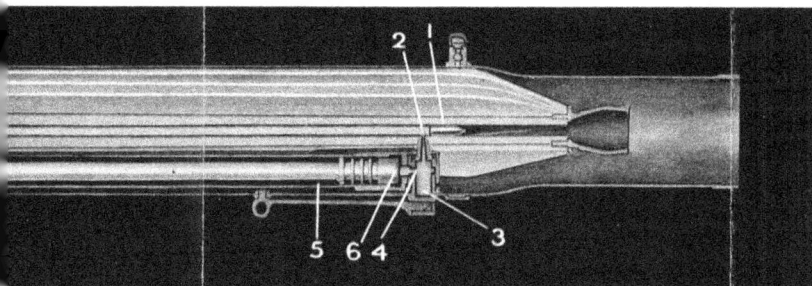

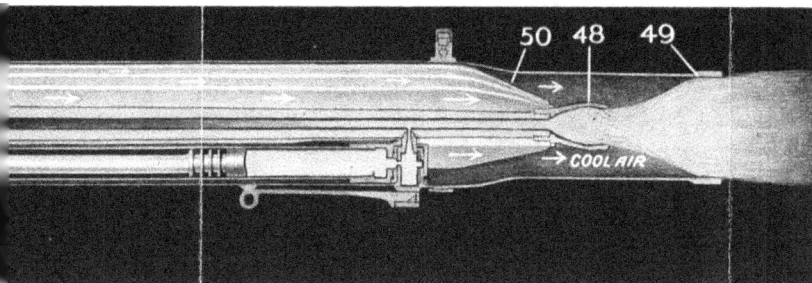

INDEX TO PLATES

www.ingramcontent.com/pod-product-compliance
Lightning Source LLC
Chambersburg PA
CBHW020953030426
42339CB00004B/81